Enyoing this book?
Please leave a review. I would be happy to receive a feedback and your opinion.

Thanks for your support.

Godensholter Strasse 84
26655 Westerstede
Germany
sandrafrers@gmail.com

Made in United States
Troutdale, OR
04/30/2025

31025176R00066